LESBIANS IGNITED

*

by Carolyn Gammon

gynergy books

Copyright © Carolyn Gammon, 1992

ISBN 0-921881-21-5
Cover Design: Catherine Matthews
Book Design: Sibyl Frei
Printer: Best Gagné Book Manufacturers Inc.
Printed & Bound in Canada using union labour

With thanks to The Canada Council for its generous support.

Thanks to the following for kind permission to quote from their work: Rule, Jane: A Hot-Eyed Moderate, (Naiad Press, 1985) by permission of the author and the publisher (p. 27). The author gratefully acknowledges The Women's Encyclopedia of Myths and Secrets as a source of invaluable reference for "Ode to Wise Blood" (p. 41).

Some of the poems in this collection have appeared in the following publications: Off Our Backs, We Shall Not be Silenced, Prism International, Simone de Beauvoir Newsletter. "On Reading Sexual Politics" was previously published in Dykewords (Women's Press, 1990). "Packing" appeared in Conditions 17 (New York, 1990). "Breaking the Rules," "Overseas Funeral," "One Poem to Avoid Another," and "To A Friend of Fourteen Years" were previously published in Our Lives (Second Story Press, 1991).

gynergy books
P.O. Box 2023
Charlottetown, PEI
Canada C1A 7N7

Canadian Cataloguing in Publication Data
Gammon, Carolyn, 1959-
  Lesbians ignited

  Poems.
  ISBN 0-921881-21-5
  I. Title.

PS8563.A66L47   C811'.54   C92-098671-4
PR9199.3.G36L47 1992

INTRODUCTION

I write for lesbians. I do not pretend to aspire to a "greater" public. Lesbians *are* at large, in every culture, community and country. Our presence, in the hundreds of millions, is enough of an audience.

I write for the laydyke and in doing so, try to keep my work accessible. Poetry has become an academic scare-word. Yet it is poetry which has come down to us through the ages in a very lesbian way, mouth to mouth, lips to lips. It is this oral tradition which saved Sappho's work from disappearing. As children, nursery rhymes are recited to us, and many peoples use oral storytelling to this day to preserve their language and culture. I consider this book a collection of oral pieces to be read aloud, shared with a room full, a field full, a bed full of dykes.

My grandmother told me stories. Life for her was a series of identifiable stories strung together. I grew up watching her arthritic milking hands gesticulate as she passed on to me a love and respect for biography and narrative. I have always been a diarist, a recorder; some of my poems are simply snapshots.

In my lesbian feminist political work I have tried to address personally and collectively, patterns of covert and overt discrimination by race, disability, class or age, which I inevitably see around me or am part of perpetrating. Audre Lorde has said: "To acknowledge privilege is the first step in making it available for wider use" (*A Burst of Light*). I try daily to acknowledge my white, middle-class, able-bodied privileges. These attempts have recently begun to inform and filter through to my poetry. Poetry *is* political. I can now laugh at the Creative Writing professor who told me to "get off a soapbox." It is a slippery but necessary place to be if we are to transform society.

Agendas happen. A gay activist is murdered in Montreal—this cannot go unrecorded. I learn about female ejaculation for the first time, this too cannot go unrecorded. Lesbians have a great deal of recording to do to make up for the millennia of repression of our collective memory, and for the personal ignorance which most of us suffer often for the first decades of our lives. We must un-learn heterosexist patriarchal values and try to forge and practise our own values. Conflicts arise and these too must be recorded.

Much of my work deals with lesbian sexual politics. I use sex as a lens through which we can view many aspects of our lives. I question the prioritizing of the hetero-marriage model—the couple and monogamy, even while often living and celebrating this model. I try to demystify lesbian sexual practices through information sharing and explicit sex talk. In the tradition of Joan Nestle, I want us to consider the political implications of our desires and discuss, rather than gloss over, the contradictions. I want to (not *all* the time) take the pink cadillac out of sex and write about a domestic erotica which infuses the everyday. To do this, I choose common currency sex terms like fuck and cunt which you can find on public bathroom walls or hear whispered coarsely while labia flap in your face. And I want to sit down to a cup of tea, a batch of dildo fuck muffins, to chat and laugh.

Dykes have a lot of talking to do, a lot of catching up to do. I offer *Lesbians Ignited* as one bite of the muffin, one bit of the conversation.

Carolyn Gammon

ACKNOWLEDGEMENTS

The first anglophone lesbian publication in Montreal, printed in 1973, was entitled *Long Time Coming*. And so this collection has been. As a result, there are many people to acknowledge and thank: Frances Firth Gammon, my mother, who bore a baby dyke and continues to nurture an adult one; Ina Rimpau, who was a constant source of encouragement, conversation, cuddles and cuntal inspiration for this book; Bina Freiwald and Robert Martin, professors at Concordia University, who showed courage in taking on my work and spent many interesting and valuable hours in debate, patiently helping me to hone my writing; Anne Cameron who offered professional support at a time I most needed it, and an ongoing friendship and exchange so vital between Canadian lesbian writers; the Canada Council who, during a very conservative era, provided funding for this very lesbian project; and *gynergy books* who have often supported my work and who have helped see this project through to completion.

I would like to thank the members of the Lesbian Studies Coalition of Concordia and the Lesbian Writers Group of Montreal, especially Marusia Bociurkiw who offered detailed editorial help; individually and collectively you have listened, given feedback and told me my poetry needed to be heard.

Thank you's to: Mary Danckert in Australia, for your long distance love, poetry and cross-continental lesbian connection; to Rosemary Ray, for bringing me out as a political dyke; to my sister, Jennifer Douglas, for saying so excitedly when I first told you of my lesbian lover: "When can I meet my sister-in-law!?"

To all the friends and lovers whose conversations, letters, photographs, poetry, artwork, videos, and political commitment have inspired me; your presence during this "long time coming" has pushed my lesbian herizons and served as the backdrop for this collection ... you are all here in *Lesbians Ignited*.

To all the lesbians and women

who have inspired me.

TABLE OF CONTENTS

COMMON GROUND
    BODY MEMORY   11
    BREAKING THE RULES   13
    PHANTOM MOON   16
    ONE POEM TO AVOID ANOTHER   18
    TO A FRIEND OF FOURTEEN YEARS   21
    OVERSEAS FUNERAL   25
    DEAR BETTY   27
    NEW BRUNSWICK, SUMMER '87   28

DYKEBLOOD
    BASIC FEMINIST LESSONS: MAN-HATING   31
    I WILL NEVER STOP   34
    AT THE HAPPY HEARTS CAMPGROUND   35
    AT A WOMYN'S FESTIVAL   38
    DYKE MEETS MODERN MEDICINE   39
    ODE TO WISE BLOOD   41
    DYKEBLOOD   42
    FUCKING DYKES   44

AT 11 O'CLOCK, I ATE MY HEART
    TIME TO TALK   47
    WHEN YOU CALLED   48
    ROSEMARY   49
    LOVE MUSCLE   51
    AT 11 O'CLOCK, I ATE MY HEART   53
    HOW TEETH CAN SPARK   54
    WASHING HER CLOTHES   55
    WE SHARE A DRINK   55
    WAYS OF MISSING   56
    BREAKING   59
    OTHER DESTINATIONS   60
    MORE THAN YOU CAN DREAM   61
    ANGER THAT HEALS   65

GYNAEVORES

PACKING	71
GYNAEVORES	73
BUTCH FEM IDENTITY CRISIS	75
ON READING *SEXUAL POLITICS*	78
BAD LESBIAN SEX	79
TUNAFISH OR ROSEMARY?	82
A PRESSING NEED	83
AT THE FEMALE EJACULATION WORKSHOP	84
CAMPING, SAGUENAY LAC ST-JEAN	87
INA	88
WHO'S WATCHING?	89
LABIA-LAUGHING	90
SATURDAY SHOPPING	92
DILDO FUCK MUFFINS	94

COMMON GROUND

∗

BODY MEMORY

body
the space between
finger and footprints
hair roots and tips
tongue and cheek
lips and lips

body holds
the sting of a browbending cold
the chafing heat of an August beach

body holds
blood
surging and crashing
on vaginal walls

body holds
the flesh-moment

mind holds
body-memory
times and times punched into the factory
the time I first touched my clitoris
the time rape came expectedly

first times, many times
memories without choice

Standing at a window
mind leans out
follows a dark coat up the street
skirts a snowbank
catches a flight to Australia

body stays
arms taut against the pane

body
naked
exposed ribs
small wrists
spread and solid legs

body
burdened
as mind
re-members

BREAKING THE RULES

Hugs were for
greetings and partings

Hands were held
for crossing the street

Tears were for
coffins being lowered

Affection meant
dough-boys in the chicken stew
the warm smell of yeasty rolls
fresh salmon, salt cod fishcakes
that extra piece of strawberry-rhubarb pie

a good game of crib
(except on Sundays) or playing 45's
with Sadie, Annie and the girls
the flowered deck worn thin

We never touched
we chatted a teacup away
never held hands
played a good hand of crib
never kissed
though the hugs lingered
as you grew older

    ✳ ✳ ✳

You're ninety-nine,
in the hospital,

Your arms are not flung
to greet me

I sit beside you
from the first moment
I take your hand
cool, tissue-soft

I hold it
caress it
compare your blue bulged veins
to my green flatter ones

I fondle the plain gold ring
worn 79 years

I remember
your hands
so deftly folding
two halves of a deck
how they carried a late breakfast tray
to two lazy granddaughters in bed
tea slopped like an angry sea

Your hands
are the only part of you
I fully recognize

They've removed your teeth
your tongue too swollen
to talk or swallow

"Do you know who I am Grannie?"

"Yaaa"

Good
then I'll tell you
'bout all the poems I've written
from stories you've told me
how you'd recite

verse after verse by Longfellow
and one called "After the Ball"
and I'll tell you
how your hands are strong
still
strong milking hands

"Yaaa"
and I'll tell you

but I'm not sure
you hear me Grannie
or see me

So I'll just hold your hand
press it
hold it
and cry when your fingertips
gently press my palm

I'd like to
clamber past the bar on the bed
wrap you in my arms

but that's really not in the family rules
and the nurse just might come in
but let's pretend we did it Grannie

Let's pretend
together
we broke the Gammon rules

PHANTOM MOON

Backpacks thrown on split-paint dory slats
we paid 25 p. for a ferry
which would not return for days

We met that day in early June
"Spend the full moon on an island," she had said
making an occasion of the moon

Our awaiting barn
was jabbed on the slant of an ocean hill
we burned dry lobster pots and slabs of turf
to boil the pot of periwinkles
picked out tiny salted meats with twigs

Full moon eve
we stripped and swam in frigid waters
to a dozen-sheep island
I climbed a boulder, pulled her after me
we sang

Swam back in pelting rain
drops, popped off the surface
slung a slow mist over the swells
from a few feet, I could barely see her

At shore the torrent warmed our bodies
as we climbed through high wet reeds

Full moon night
we stoked a vigil with bricks of peat
climbed out our window

Across the island, two miles we walked
Irish fiddlers played all night

And because she did not dance with me
and I would not ask
I took a man
to drink and dance, put arms around me

In a thistle-down dawn
we trailed back to our barn
phantom full moon above

ONE POEM TO AVOID ANOTHER

for Jennifer

Two women
biological sisters

red hair
when we're together
blazons our sisterhood

voices so much alike
we fool friends
even Mum, on the phone

we have learned to swim
in the same waves, been beaten
by the same leather strap
recited the same prayers
to Grannie upstairs
counselled beneath the same blanket-house
over the hot air register
climbed the same sticky sap pines

Two girls grown
one lesbian
one married to a man

Can we find
a common ground?

* * *

When you visit
my lesbian space

Large mauve vulvic flowers poster my bedroom wall
Lesbenglün, Lust auf München, on Ina's
Hello-you-cute-cunt messages
tacked to the bulletin board
Dykes to Watch Out For
on the back of the flush
The music of Phranc, Lucie "Blue"
or Casselberry-Dupreé

When you visit this space
where few men come
your husband may enter
I will not ask
that your wedding rings
be left in a jar by the door

When I enter
your married space

>   Ring the doorbell
>   that no longer bears our shared name
>   Family photos framed
>   in the master bedroom
>   The baby's album
>   at afternoon tea
>   A bicycle-built-for-two
>   raised seat and handlebars up front

When I enter this space
where few dykes go
I will not shrug off my lesbianism
like a coat to be hung in the closet

   * * *

Eric will soon be one
he will soon be two, three, four
he will soon be aware

that this visiting aunt
shares her life with women

So I write now
to let you know
I will send amazon alphabets
picture books which show
two daddies, three mummies
I will say the "L" word
in his presence
And I will be with my lover
as I always am
evident, intimate
in front of his asking eyes

Let's decide in advance
Let's not wait for
a scene
when I'm four thousand miles
from home

We have a chance
one of those small
personal decisions
that create a society
shall we find
a common ground?

TO A FRIEND OF FOURTEEN YEARS

I am outraged
though you'll not see
this raw angry woman
I won't arrive at your door with an acid tongue
I won't send letter bombs
but I am outraged

Through the years
I thought I'd made the necessary adjustments
dropped friends I had to
separated past from present
like yolk from the white
leaving me only family back home

and you

who say you value our friendship
a friendship so airtight
it leaves no room for me
to hold hands with my lover
on your Island roads

We did not FUCK
in front of you
or your family
or your friends
We did not strip on your front lawn
we did not neck, slobber, rub cunts
or even
kiss
(as you and your husband did
 in front of us
 on the open ferry road)

We did not
bring placards, megaphones
We did not
spraypaint women's symbols on the dock
We did not
compare clams to vulvas at the supper table

We held hands
held hands

   * * *

We've been friends
fourteen years
agreed all our mutual influences
our coaches, idols,
our crushes
all all all
were lesbian

You have said
you could have
gone either way

Then
in six months
you find a man
and GOD
dip into the gelid Island water
come out
born again
better than me

"This is our house"
"We'll be the gossip of the community"
"It isn't normal"

Listen
Listen to your Christian words—
there you'll find an "abomination to the Lord"

    * * *

I'm tired
too tired
to disinter this
once again
this simple act of holding hands

I visited before with lovers
we held hands in your living room
this passed—green light

I thought
I thought
at this most basic level
the borders of respect were drawn
But a living room is not a lawn
a lawn is not an Island road
hands held are not just
hands held
gestures of affection are not
normal
in a living room yes
on a road no
for you yes
for us no
yes
no
I'm tired

tired of finding myself
crying on holiday

    * * *

Fortunately for me
the outraged woman
comforts the bawling one
You can have
your gay-damned Island

You can have
your stingy invitations
that come with open arms and loopholes

we may even exchange
civil correspondence
after time has sifted my anger
to a dust so fine
you might only sneeze on it

but you can't have my friendship
not on those terms

OVERSEAS FUNERAL

Your father has died

"I would come with you
but it isn't the time"
                    I say

    I see us at Heathrow
    the smiles and embracing
    you push me forward
    proudly as always
    holding my hand, saying
    "This is my lover, Carolyn"

    I see the offense
    etched on their faces
    as they tactfully back up
    maybe offering a fingertip
    or two ... I hear them think
    "As if a death isn't enough"

    At the funeral parlour
    you and me standing near the open casket
    arm around waist
    and no one approaching
    the corpse, or us

    At the ceremony
    family files to the front pew
    husbands, wives seated somberly together
    and us, during head-bowed prayers,
    snatching glances across the church

    Who will ride with the hearse?
    What if you insist
    and there ensues a loud Cockney row
    in the parking lot?

Caps flung
roses trampled

At the graveside
where would we stand?
Could we hold hands
to comfort?

"It *is* the time
I want you to come
We should be together now"

Yes, maybe you're right ...

Maybe they would greet us
with open arms and, if we hadn't eaten on the plane,
offer beans on toast and tea
there'd always be that space
at the edge of the pew
or tucked on your lap
beside the driver in the hearse
Maybe they would need some extra hands
to carry bouquets to the cemetery
and there'd be a stool in the kitchen afterwards
for sandwiches and chat

It *is* the time

but your salt-and-pepper hair
and blue union jacket
have disappeared behind security
I'm sitting on a bench
wanting to pull that plane back
out of the air

and say Yes, it is the time

DEAR BETTY

For Elizabeth Brewster

In Canada we have a remarkable number of gifted and articulate women who will not be reduced to what New York or feminist presses think women want to read ... It is not a question of whether Margaret Atwood or Elizabeth Brewster are feminists but whether the women's movement is confident enough to claim their power ...

Jane Rule
A Hot-Eyed Moderate

You lived across the street
had tea with my mother
held my small fevered body when I had strep throat
always asked for a large glass of water at meals
closed your eyes upward when speaking

Your books arrived Christmas after Christmas
poems I was too young to want to read
except the one for my sister and her loose tooth
the one about my brothers, their passion for magnets

That you lived across the street, wrote about us,
reduced you in my eyes
"Poets" were supposed to be
distant fellows, living on heaths

Then, reading women's poetry
I left no room for you
There were no obvious clenched fists, lesbian symbols,
not enough of the raging feminist
I call myself and wanted to read

When Ma would tell me
"that one of yours is just like Betty's"
I wondered why and how ...

It took Jane Rule
to bring you back to me

NEW BRUNSWICK, SUMMER '87

Miraculously
we find the porch door to my parents' cottage, open
Large drops hassle us inside
We hang the candle lantern from fishnetting
spread camping mats
light the gas stove
You eat your first lobster
suckle each joint
slather the fine meat in hot garlic butter

Next day, I bring my brother
You talk philosophy and cameras
I'm glad you get along
Curled into your stomach,
I dip in and out of sleep,
your hands unconsciously tracing my face

He later asks my mother
"Why does Carolyn get such nice women
and not me?"

Well into the night
Geoff takes his scotch-soaked mind to the guest tent
we light sparklers
wave electric women's symbols along the beach,
feminist fireflies

We're not too tired to make
lobster-scotch-country-sweat-love
till night no longer holds us
At lake's edge
we watch the sun rise on the point,
rinsing our laughing, swollen vulvas

DYKEBLOOD

✳

BASIC FEMINIST LESSONS:
MAN-HATING

for Patrizia

When your lover calls
at 2 a.m. to confront you
with being a Man-Hater

Dig the sleep from your eyes, clear your throat
tell her to wait a moment while you make a hot drink
and when you've had your first sip

Ask her:
– Have I ever raped a man?
– Have I ever assaulted a man? Driven a broken bottle up his rectum?
– Have I ever smashed my fists through a man's face? Made him flee from his home to a shelter?
– Have I hoisted flashing neon cock-and-balls over Ste-Catherine Street and charged for entry?
– Have I kept men out of government?
– Have I offered them jobs at 62 cents to my dollar?
– Do I take sex-holidays and pay to fuck economically deprived, "exotic" men?
– Have I ever given a course called "Human" and used only women's texts?
– Have I ever harassed men in the streets? Come up behind, breathing hotly in one ear "I want your prick, darling"
– Have I ever taken a man to court over child custody for being heterosexual?
– Have I ever gone into the bathroom with a man's four-year-old son and made him suck on me till I come?
– Did I sexually molest my younger brothers while growing up?
– Have I ever said a man couldn't be Pope? And set up institutions to ensure it?

– Have I ever bought a plastic male blow-up doll to haul out at lesbian parties and ridicule?
– Have I ever given a party to celebrate my loving a woman and watched videos all night of men being raped?
– Have I ever thrown darts at a glossy porn shot of a man's crotch pinned up in the union shop?
– Have I ever taken a gun into a university classroom, told the women to leave, yelled man-hating slogans, and shot every man dead?

Now, take a gulp or two of tea, and ask her
for as long as she's known you
and even though you may have felt
like doing some of the above ...

HOW
    personally
        politically
           publicly
              physically
                  economically
                      sexually
                      HOW
                          concretely
                              realistically
                                  day-to-day

your Man-Hating
has manifested itself?

Have you said you will never fuck men again?
Have you stated that your apartment will be man-free?
Have you put up female images on the walls?
Have you refused to go to parties where men will be?
Have you gone to Take Back The Night marches and told men to stay at the back?
Have you mused that you'd rather not have brothers?

Have you said LESBIAN out loud while taking the Metro?
Have you made comments about "men" generically?
Have you worked politically with women only? Gone to
women "only" festivals?
Have you said you love women?

Just what sort of Man-Hating CRIMES have you committed?

If your tea has not gone cold
and she's still awake and on the phone
ask her, what then
is *SO* threatening about you hating men?

If she can answer that one
she's a feminist
and there's hope for your relationship

I WILL NEVER STOP

One a.m.
phone rings
a death? I think
accident?
my lover who just left?

I pick it up
Hello?
A twisted voice
one word
hard to my ear
"DYKE"
click
dial tone

The receiver drops
from my hand

How—
did that voice
know my number?
Has he watched in windows?
binocular eyes
across the street
Has he followed me?
been in the house already
read posters on the wall
taken my number
found keys, made copies?
Will he call again?
grab me in the back alley
as I park my bike
or jump me from behind
the shower curtain ...

And because of that
fear
that one a.m.
word
spit across phone lines, that
one beautiful word
charred to an insult

Because of that
one threat
and any
any other

I will never stop
marching in the streets
shouting in front of the courts
churches, schools
I will never stop
holding hands with lovers
on buses, in lobbies
I will never stop
writing to newspapers,
politicians
writing for students, comrades,
union sisters, for dykes,
straights, for children,
grandmothers, for lovers

for myself
I will never stop

AT THE HAPPY HEARTS CAMPGROUND

After ember-roasted potatoes
after strolling, necks craned to stars
lying naked
cocoon-close in our tiny tent

At first
you thought it was a child
getting slapped
a whimper, a cry
mixed with late night blasted music

But with time, a half hour, an hour
a raised male voice
slaps becoming thuds
you wake me

We listen
past the cricket chirps
and frog calls

"Fucking bitch, you fucking ..."
THUD, smack on flesh
then whimpering, weeping
like an animal, long-trapped
its blood running low

Another volley
I grab clothes up and out of the tent
hear your voice
"He might have a knife ...!"

Approaching the tent
we see two park wardens
two men
waiting
an hour

for the beating
to disturb the peace

"He could kill her!" I say
going for police

NO! they say
they will go with flashlights
and inquire

We stand, bare feet in wet grass
look eye to eye through the dark

"Is everything all right here?"
flashlight beam spreads over green nylon
Silence
then, male answers "Yes"

    ✷ ✷ ✷

We can't sleep
light a fire
make tea, sit close

imagine

twenty, thirty, forty
lesbians
encircling the tent
armed with self-defence

imagine
amazons
swinging neon labryses
demanding with shattering voices
that the violence
STOP

We imagine
anything

anything

as the silent campground
and holiday-earned stars
scream and stare at us

AT A WOMYN'S FESTIVAL

I saw a womon
dancing
dancing naked to bongos

Sweat poured from her head
laughter teemed from her face
her arms raised and swaying
palms strobed the setting sun behind her

and instead of breasts
she wore scars
with a live tattoo
bright leaf greens
flowing across her chest
defying the lies of porn
that breasts equal wo-man
wo-man equals breasts
I raised my arms
joined in, with this
proud dancing womon

DYKE MEETS MODERN MEDICINE

STD's
happen to other people
to prostitutes and johns
to dumb hets and gays
who don't use safes
They might even happen
to Napoleon, Meryl Streep
or the guy down the street

but not to lesbians
clean, safe-sex dykes
no cocks
no sperm
no bizarre little bacteria
hidden under penal flaps

So why do I find myself
in hospital?
Five-day fever
burning, runny cunt
swollen nodes
pain rolling down my throat
like an ostrich swallowing

When diagnosed
the doctor explained
"It is passed
　from tip of the penis
　　directly to the squamo-columnar junction of the cervix"

"Can it be passed,"
I asked politely
"From cervix to cervix?"
Her brows furrowed
she leafed through books
she thought through ten years of education

and lastly she taxed her imagination
all to no avail
Her medical expertise
just could not stretch
from one cervix to another

I did have chlamydia though
she couldn't deny
so I left
with enough drugs
to keep me going in yeast infections
for the following year

ODE TO WISE BLOOD

Earliest humanity
believed menstrual blood coagulated into new life
Maoris and Africans thought human souls
were made of menstrual blood

The Greeks called it "supernatural red wine"
and the Celts, "red or royal mead"
One Norse god bathed in a river of menstrual blood
from the giantesses

The Chinese gained immortality by drinking
red yin juice
Egyptian pharaohs deified their dead
with amulets of our menstrual blood
In Mycenae, the word for "the people"
was "mother blood"

The Bible calls it "blood the flower"
or fruit of the womb
and Adam means "bloody clay"

Some called it
wise blood
moon dew
elixir of immortality

and the Goddess-given menstrual calendar
with thirteen annual lunar months
was established by Chinese women
three thousand years ago

    * * *

That's a lot of history
to ignore
every twenty-eight days

DYKEBLOOD

Giving blood
campus centre lobby
I look around
one, two, three, four
dykes I know
giving blood

All those
feminist corpuscules
anti-patriarchal plasma
disease fighting cells

Dykeblood
the safest blood to give

flowing out over Montreal
answering sirens
perhaps for a guy
split by a beam on the Jacques Cartier bridge
as he cruised home from date-rape
or dykeblood
whisked to the 20th floor of Ville-Marie
to a man, still stuffed in his suit
who has spent millions
to strip the Amazon rain forests
pour acid on our maples
dykeblood
arriving with paramedics
when the next army helicopter
goes down

   ✶ ✶ ✶

At the Hôtel Dieu
A-positive dykeblood
pumping into the waiting veins

of a lesbian hemorrhaging
while her lover
battles in the hall
for the right to enter the room

Our dykeblood
running out of us
to Metro Frontenac
where Joe Rose with his pink hair
is being stabbed and kicked to death

I hear "FUCKING FAGGOT FUCKING FAGGOT"
and suffocate and suck blood
with each blow to the abdomen

And our blood arrives too late
or our blood arrives too soon
or not at all

I want to ask the kind old woman
who fastens a band-aid to the crook of my arm
"Could I have my pint please?
  ... and hers, and hers"

I want to gather all that dykeblood
spill it on the snow, on the cement
where Joe Rose fell

and yell
and yell
and yell

FUCKING DYKES

I grew up
hating
the word
lesbian

hating
the word
dyke

On the field hockey team
a friend and teammate
backed out of an elevator crying
she'd heard that Mona
was "one of them"
and would not risk
the ride down three floors

On long van trips
the girls discussed boyfriends
who made noise with whom
in the next residence room
was it the Pill or I.U.D
and who might be
a lezzie

Though not guilty
I remained silent

I was so
careful
those words
were never used
on me

Now
skating
with my lover
Parc LaFontaine
a bright, cold
snappy day
laughing, chatting
hand in hand
in unison
we propel our blades
slantways
carving sharp golden angles
on the ice

"FUCKING DYKES"

we are buzzed by
jolted

"YES!"
"YES!"
"THAT'S IT"
"YOU'VE GOT IT RIGHT!"

and we skate on
the day
as bright and cold
as before

At 11 O'Clock, I Ate My Heart

✶

TIME TO TALK

for Monika

We have not pretended
that sex is as easy as animals
who know how to rut

we have left
"groping in the dark"
to back seat drive-ins
of our pasts

We have talked
tasted, touched and said
yes, this feels good
no, not that

or masturbated
to show each other
just how

(At the campsite
on the outjut of land
you watched in the sun
as I pulled lips apart
talked, stroked
and we agreed for the lesson
not to be sexual
but it happened anyway)

We have spoken
with other lesbians
heard them say what they like

(At the solstice party
when we pulled out
On Our Backs
asked and answered:
"I come inside"
"I want clitoral always"
"I like my ass")

We have charted our bodies
with flashlight and speculum

I know my way as I travel
to cup your protruding cervix
finger the folded, clutched
vaginal walls

You've spoken to my tongue
urged her along your clit shaft
told her to spread your lips
purple and full

We've taken time
time to talk
hours, afternoons
dusks, dawns
time when we might come
or not

WHEN YOU CALLED

when you called

on an urge

to tell me

you loved me

i was masturbating

and didn't

answer

the

 p

 h

 o

 n

 e

ROSEMARY

At the dance it was physical
you had to have me

I biked to your place
nearly catching my wheel in a streetcar track

I'd never felt
such vise-grip strength
your pelvis
pinning me to the bed
lesbian sex, snapped
like static on a cold night

And with that strength
you massaged the knot that gripped me
years of hormones teemed into my gut

That night
I knew nothing about you
nothing but you

    * * *

Days and nights are happening
Rosemary
and sometimes I can't believe this is mine
I was not prepared
to find it so good

When I consider your body
warm, full-breasted
meeting my sleep
a wave moving sand

when you're stretched high
telling me to go on

I risk to lose myself

A body
can only hold so much
before bursting
like milkweed in the wind

LOVE MUSCLE

You rock me
like a cradle in the utmost boughs

You hold me
like a cabin holding on a wind-swept point
your hands, large-knuckled, soft
Years you fought while I crawled
laboured while I made puzzles

While you were marching for lesbian rights
I was dropping balls through a hoop

Unknown to us
I struggled to catch up
travelled, opened my eyes
put a big house behind me

Then
we meet and love—
those years dissolve
sand through an hourglass

Except
I cry more often
maul you with moods

And sometimes I wonder why you bother
there are so many other women
who don't need their strength instilled

One night we discuss the threadbare blanket
I spread on our time together
I cry and there you are, rocking me,
tending me with your years

"Wait for me to catch up"
You wrap arms around me

And I'll hold you
like an iron bar above my head
all that love muscle
to strengthen me

AT 11 O'CLOCK, I ATE MY HEART

You, from rivetting, me from Stores
takes us five minutes each
to cross the plant

We choose a time
meet in the bathroom
I give you a gingerbread bear

We didn't really fight
just disagreed
but missed our toilet-stall kiss
as I left in a rush

Back at my machine
a thin layer of tears
blurs the saw blades and flying metal chips

Late shift is no time to cry

Later, in aluminium-blacked coveralls
you appear
hand me a packet wrapped in a paper towel

A candied gingerbread heart
you'd eaten round the bear

I pocketed my little packet
and sitting with the guys for tea

at 11 o'clock
I ate my heart

HOW TEETH CAN SPARK

Thanks for this chance
sex
without the questions
what next, when next

The "one-night stand"
so over-used, abused
by bad movies, bad jokes
Can we reclaim
even that?

It seems so

Sure
I learned some things new
how teeth can spark my skin
how a woman's full stomach breathes
like a warm animal between my legs
how a needy cunt beats rhythmically

how to take friendship
and make love with it

I liked it after
in the shower
soap smoothed on my ass
then sitting in the kitchen
your face in my hands
at my breasts

the coffee tasted good

I like the smile
my roommate tells me not to lose

WASHING HER CLOTHES

I washed her clothes today
a huge laundry, four washers, two dryers
eight dollars in change

pulled pure colours from the dryer
the hot pink shirt that bites over her breasts
the tight green pants that mold around her bike seat
the checkered jacket for the bars

I washed her clothes today
and folded the blue and white stripes
that first seduced me

WE SHARE A DRINK

mouth to mouth
cool silent stream

"I wonder," she says
"if it's like being at the breast"

sucking-soft
lips pulled like taffy

WAYS OF MISSING

I

WELCOME LIGHT

At the airport
for once goons don't shout
when we embrace cry kiss
as if lesbianism is alright
if it's goodbye

We stand five millimetres away
lips squished on plexiglass
looking through a diving mask
we are tropical fish

I make a paper airplane
fly I-love-you over the security wall
hope they don't nab you in duty-free

Driving back from Mirabel
I think of our pre-parting fights and cuddles
as if good-bye means we don't care
so we played at breaking up
played at staying together forever

An inopportune case of candida
kept us from fucking the hurt away

Coming home without you
your boots in the stairwell
a welcome light you left on for me

The missing is worse at first
becomes habit
I put your boots out of sight
turn the welcome light on for myself

check the mail
listen for the long-distance beep

We are tropical fish
drifting with wave swells
swimming brightly past one another

//

Like a raw nerve in a tooth
I never knew I could miss this much

I constantly refrain
from picking up the phone

I say your name
aloud, in public
by mistake

At the supermarket
I scan the aisles, choose, replace
check out with an empty cart

Your photo on my bedside wall:
bare-breasted, level gaze
hand relaxed behind your head
an evening sun tossing
driftwood shadows on your face
and nipples

The photo is damp
and wrinkled from kisses
that only a stuffed lobster has witnessed

I organize
do desk work
roller skate
make myself take ice-cream
at the dyke café

... And the longer you stay away

the more my nights fill
with dreams of women
other than you
I make love to

///

I must say it

I miss your body

I miss your hand pranking at my snatch

I miss the unexpected twitch on my breast

I miss your cold fingers snuggling down the crack of my ass

I miss your weighty, ebbing lips

I miss your tongue swelling over mine

I miss your kiss when I ask you to come down on me

And more

I miss your large roaming breasts

I miss the impact of our hips

I miss that numbing flood through my cunt

I miss your body

and I can't wait

BREAK
ING

Now that we've said
we're breaking up
                    down, a-part
this
is with me all the time

Like a sore foot
a headache, a cloudy day
something that isn't quite right

Once I was told
I had cells changing to cancerous
on my cervix, and my life split
into before and after knowing

Before, I could miss you or not
think of you or not

After, the day ticks by
like a metronome

I-love-you-
I-love-you-
not?

I am a comic strip character
with a clean, clear hole
blown through her middle
yet, I keep walking about
                      normally

    (Headache
      cancer cells
      before
      after
      daisies
      bullet hole
      breaking
      up?)

OTHER DESTINATIONS

In Gorlizter Park, where the East used to be
November holds bright yellow leaves

Eggs filled with paint
splatter clean walls

I write postcards
with red ink

I'm in love in Berlin
breaking up in Montreal

I walk crunching coloured bits
of wall underfoot

Climb a watchtower
listen to Tracy Chapman in a Kreuzberg cafe

In the Turkish bath we
oil, massage, brush, soap and cream
each others bodies
Telephone turns to ice on my ear
  I don't want to be your lover anymore
  I'm moving out

Egg breaks
red paint splats and drips

I put stamps on cards
mail to "Other Destinations"

In her apartment
coal carried five floors
slowly warms the kitchen

MORE THAN YOU CAN DREAM

for Katharina

In January
I'll love you
hard as ice
frozen waterfalls
solid curtained cold
sure as rock
you could climb
with ice picks and crampons
my love captured
maybe for centuries

In February
I'll love you
sure as a frozen pond
where I skate
cutting ice angles in your name
I'll make a snow statue
chiselled blue silver
rubbed transparent
kids can slip and slide
on its base and limbs

In March
I'll love you
a vein cracked open
blue and running
In the crunch of frozen mud
rain freezing fast
wrapping every twig
We'll taste thin maple sap
leave tracks in the snow

In April
I'll love you

with the freeing of the river
fast passage of ice floes
rush of logs and branches
The returning of the heron
The incessant melt and drip
The river
flooding from its banks

In May
I'll love you
a fiddlehead harvest
steamed and served
with butter and salt
On your table
three plucked lady's slippers
pink, yellow, white
And we will eat
delicately

In June
I'll love you
a lake
spring cold and shocking
The pebbles warm
beneath your ass
as I sit and stroke you
towel-covered on an empty beach
Still cold at night
I'll love you with blankets
stories of sturgeon
and shooting stars

In July
I'll love you
hot
Oiling your toes, feet, calves, thighs
massaging sun into your back and breasts
I'll shade your face

feed you cold lemonade from my lips
tease nipples with ice
Under water, I'll dive between your legs
The beach too hot to walk on
we'll run fast to shade
and under the poplars
kiss

In August
I'll love you
gathering daisy and goldenrod
wild rose and everlastings
We'll choose a silky corn stalk
play between bales of hay
In the hum of bees
crickets and night noises of bull frogs
like living creatures
wild, necessary

In September
I'll love you
pedalling by the river in wind
willows bent and blowing
By canoe
waves splashing the bow
where you lean to pour tea
as we lunch midstream
drifting toward the cattailed bank

In October
I'll love you
reds and yellows
screaming on the hills
Overhead, a V of honking geese
In wool sweater sweat
and rake-made blisters
I'll kiss your hands
We'll make piles of leaves

maple and elm
push each other in
and fall on top

In November
I'll love you
a long scarf
thrown over both shoulders
Hand in your gloved hand
cold sidewalks rush us home
to hot showers
body brushes
candles and dry wine
Facing winter
I'll love you fiercely

In December
I'll love you
with cocoa, gifts and poems
With the finest snow
flinging sun at the kitchen window
With the first snowball
struck on a tree trunk
We'll make angels in the snow
Beneath winter clothes
our bodies warm and steaming

On the thirteenth month
I'll love you
by the moon
when I come
sure as a shadow
soft and strong
inside and out
more than you can dream

ANGER THAT HEALS

You touch me
inside
where other lovers could not go
You excite me, scare me
laugh and cry me
You jump around my heart
like children 'round the mulberry bush

And then sweet one
you speak harshly, criticize, urge me
to be someone I might like to be
but I'm not her yet
I've only just seen the inside you've touched
and I'm not closing my eyes
for the scary parts

When you love me with your eyes and lips
anything is possible
When you grab my collar, shake me
throw anger like lightning

I flash back
to the parking lot
a father's fist in my face
the bedroom,
pants down, leather to flesh

I know your anger comes from love
but the girl in the parking lot does not
she's waiting for the next blow
she's lived years with this already
and knows there will always be a next one

Can we love without anger?

Dykes in the street marching at night
"Cut it out or cut it off!"
"No more patriarchy, no more SHIT!"

But we are not the enemy
and when the street becomes our living room
the girl comes back with an unclenched fist
nose bleeding on her yellow shirt

We must find other ways
to teach-love
one another

With love so strong
there will be strained muscles
sex screaming between us

> Remember at night
> your head in my arms
> one turns the other follows

Love work
is done with heavy machinery
scoops and shovels in our voices
facing each other
on either end of the couch
steel flashing from our eyes
as the beams are constructed
then a clasping of hands
when the job is done
and each day, anew
the work begins

> Sometimes at dawn
> I wake   We are apart in bed
> You stir, turn and dive for my arms
> a dolphin back to warm sea

We can love
again and again
We work
you at your desk
I at mine
a room of serious intent between us
cats padding the hall

We love
on the same continent
in a way we cannot
with an ocean between us

When I first loved you
I thought it was a fairy tale
such miracles happen only to princesses

You opened the book
I stepped into the pages

"Come look," you said
"There's a cobblestone path,
a rainbow, a treasure
and ..."

But sometimes I can't believe
not in you
not in our story

The girl in the parking lot
blood still dripping
doesn't believe in fairytales
she doesn't believe

The next blow is coming to get you

Love
again and again

clasp hands
roll together
eyes like steel
anger that heals
anger that heals

Love me
I love you
love me
I love you love me

Baby
what happens
on the next page?

GYNAEVORES

✶

PACKING

I'm packing my bags
for travel

I've got one long slim pink cotton tote-bag
for one long lavender
1 1/4 inch on one end, 1 3/8 inch on the other
Double Venus Rising

I've packed a couple of flexible
silicone rubber dildos
for the red leather harness
with additional opening

The Eager Beaver with vibrating tongue
and pearl-size beads to rotate the shaft,
I've slid into a side pocket
next the G-spotter
and the a.p.d.

I won't forget my Ben Wa Balls
14-karat gold—they pack small

Let's see
multi-coloured condoms
water-soluble lube
a couple of lube inserts
just in case

Clove soap in my cosmetics bag
almond oil, rosewater
and a lickable amaretto cream

I've got *GAIA'S Guide*
to find my way around
and *Sapphistry* for those spare moments

I'm a touch worried
about crossing the border

but I'm ready
to go!

GYNAEVORES

(or two Dykes take their summer vacation in the Maritimes)

On the briny strands of Cape Breton
off the misty shoals of Meat Cove
through the patient fogs of the Ceildhi Trail
to coniferous stands and perennial bogs

In the atavistic summer of '88
in a duo they came
combing the beaches for mussel and clam
crouching about damp fires at night
bathing their lithe or lumbering flesh
in fresh water falls
icy salt surf

In open fields they played
entertaining their limbs
in vast quantities of sun

In dark woods they trod
seeking the salamander, snake, and frog

They were ungainly
their bulbous and hairy breasts
beating together in furious song
leg-long labia
slapping wet earth where they walked
excessive juices washing the land
forming natural dykes in their wake

They were female
yet coupled in mating
their unearthly screams
shattering the sullen skies

Wherever they went
the locals scattered
fearing their way of life
was ending

Their presence was unexpected
their departure, celebrated

Gynaevores!

BUTCH FEM IDENTITY CRISIS

I'm a fem
I have long red hair
and chatty wrists
which twirl as I talk
with my high, sometimes whiney
voice

I'm a fem
quick to cry
easy to soothe
with hot cocoa
and caresses

I'm a fem
I prowl the lingerie department at the Bay
choose a silk black bustier

posed in front of a full length mirror
my pouting pussy says Meooww—
come and wet me

HEY! BUT WHO YOU CALLING FEM?!

I'm a butch
One-hundred-fifty-pound bench press
butch

I don't "modulate" my voice
in public

I wear a made-to-measure
black suit coat
carry a billfold in the back-ass pocket
of my tight Levis

I'm a butch
make no mistake
I pack a dildo
sheath it and lube it
and use it on my baby

THAT PIECE YOU'RE PACKING'S NOT MUCH OF A
   COCK
AND THAT'S NO HARNESS, IT'S A "WAIST BRACELET"

DIDN'T I SEE YOU ONCE IN A PINK NEGLIGEE
SPLIT UP THE SIDE?

AND THAT BENCH PRESS—
YOUR GIRLFRIEND CAN TOTE YOU AROUND
SLUNG OVER HER SHOULDER
ANYTIME

Okay, okay
so I'm a butch-in-the-streets ...

I do the fuck-off walk
carry my fists ball-breaking stiff

My strides are long and fast
I'd fall off the curb in heels

... and I'm a fem-in-the-sheets

That packed dildo?
I change the sheath, offer it to my Hunk and say:
use this on me
please ...
spread on the kitchen table
she eases into my floral ass
with lots of K-Y gel

WHAT'S THIS 'BOUT YOU EJACULATING
A PUDDLE ON THE FLOOR,
SAVING IT IN A THIMBLE

WHAT SORT OF
BUTCH-FEM-BUTCH
FEM-BUTCH-FEM
ARE YOU ANYWAY?

I'm a fem
I have long red hair
and chatty wrists
that pump a hundred-fifty pound bench press

I'm a butch
make no mistake
I pack a slim two-fingered
pale lavender dildo
I like to take it in the ass
with lots of cream

ON READING *SEXUAL POLITICS*

How to explain
to Kate Millett
to myself

while reading
a Norman Mailer extract
where a woman gets fucked
to a pulp

How to explain
while reading
I reached down
into my pants and stroked my clitoris
wet fingers and probed inside

How to explain
I went back to his words
and working faster
jammed my cunt on the corner of the chair—

came gloriously
head on the open book

> "The prevailing culture ...
> is saturated with sexuality ...
> that simultaneously
> tantalizes and repels."

Thank-you Adrienne Rich

BAD LESBIAN SEX

shhhh
don't talk about it

don't talk about the time
on the first night
a lover tore your hand away from her clit
turned her back on you

or the time she didn't want to
you rubbed up anyway
she said she felt raped

don't tell
that sometimes sex is a chore
an exchange of goods
a way to end a fight

don't mention
how often you found her dry
how often you faked coming
so sex would stop

don't for heaven's sake
count the times you fucked unsafely
didn't ask how many men she'd fucked
and how recently
lapped menstrual blood
without a question
shared vag juices with yeast infection
kissed with herpes on its way

don't say
how many of us are abused
by family, by strangers
how we carry this with us
like fingerprints

don't write a poem
about stopping a lover mid-rhythm
it reminded you of being raped
years before

don't say how many of us need to be drunk
to be sexual
need to shoot up before making a move

don't tell a soul
about the time you saw
one dyke bend her chick backward
over the bar like a rag doll

don't tell
about your one-night-stand
who flew from bed in the morning
as if on fire
and though you saw her many times after
you never mentioned "it" again

don't let others know
that for three years with a lover
you never showed each other how
until sex hung between you like a bad joke

don't remember
how many lesbian lovers
compare you to men:
  you fuck like a man
  only a man would do that
  it was better with men

don't say
how many times you wanted to come
and couldn't
how many times your hand went numb
saliva dried up

don't say
how many dykes you avoid in public
because you've fucked
how many friendships ended
with sex

don't
don't
say

shhhh

TUNAFISH OR ROSEMARY?

In class
my fingers
passed innocently
under my nose

and a strong odour
from there rose

"Rosemary!"
I thought with a sneak

but in a flash
the time it took for smell
to fly to brain and circle once
I knew it wasn't her at all!
but tunafish
from a sandwich at lunch

Somehow
I still enjoyed
passing my fingers
under my nose
tunafish though it was

A PRESSING NEED

Unfolding the long crossed legs
of the ironing board, I slip
a vaginal insert vibrator into
the tight crotch of my panties

run the wire to my pocket
put the buzz on low

At perma press
I hum and swing my hips
in large slow sweeps

For wools and cottons
I add steam
cross my legs
and squeeze

Half way through a difficult collar
a pressing need develops

The clothes will have to wait

AT THE FEMALE EJACULATION WORKSHOP

Well—WHY THE HELL NOT?!
Of course we can ejaculate
or fountain, or gush, or hit-the-wall
or emit spontaneous urethral eruptions
whatever you want to *call* it
of *course* we can

Just because it's been hushed up for years
centuries, make that millenia
just because Hirschfeld and the boys ignored it
Kinsey denied it and Masters says it ain't so
doesn't mean we don't

So we're sitting around a tree at Michigan
about fifty dykes
and the workshop leader asks—
How many of you ejaculate?

Up go the hands
over half

How does it taste, smell, look, FEEL?
and how much and how often
and how?

More hands shot up

> "First it was with my husband
> I was ashamed to wet the bed
> and he didn't like it
> so for twenty years I held it back
> I didn't come for twenty years ...
> Now I have a woman lover—she loves it
> and I come every time
> wet the bed every time"

    "I'll tell you"
says another
    "I thought I'd been around the block
    I thought I was *really good*
    but when this lover spurts all over me
    I'm saying to myself:
    Do I ignore it? play polite?
    Do I drink it?
    Like what do I do???"

– My lover taught me
– I discovered it masturbating
– I need fingers on my G-spot, you know, reach in and up
– It takes a lot of pressure
– It takes a little
– Once I fountained with just nipple stimulation
– You've got to bear down
– I recommend Sears rubber sheets with flannel covers
– It's clear
– It doesn't taste
– It changes taste during the month
– It's *not* urine
– So what if it is?
– Once, it shot across the bed—and I mean *lengthwise*
– I love it running down my arm, I get soooo turned on

I'm sitting there
me, dyke-born, 1959
Fredericton, New Brunswick, Canada
listening to maybe ten thousand years
of hidden lesbian herstory
asking myself WHY, WHY, WHY
was it so vital to hide?

Then a voice from the back

    "I was thinking
      maybe it's a vestige

of women being able to reproduce
among ourselves
Maybe if we worked on it ..."

Silence fell under the tree at Michigan

and I went home
to work on it

CAMPING, SAGUENAY LAC ST-JEAN

spider nimbles across a twig
salmon river blurts over stones

sun sets pink behind rock and fir
wind washes leaves

kindling in a teepee waiting for fire
tea on the boil

a two-woman tent

now with the river
bare bodies splashing

now with the wind
oil and onion

now with the stars
flames juggling close conversation

now with the night
shadows stretch and settle

orange tent-glow
clitorises ignite

INA

goddess knows
I like your body
thick ass and thighs

standing in the kitchen
glued at the pelvis
the gathering of cream

the popping kisses
you send off, like tiny
flesh firecrackers

I like your crude
lesbian mouth
and how little
men mean to you

I like licking, tugging
your closed eyelids

I like how you bite
with your inner ragged
tooth edge
your nails etching my spine

I like tonguing
through your wiry pubes
to plump-ripe labia and clit

your strong, acrid
cunt-woman taste

I like how you want a hand in
long after you come
(last night
I left it there as we slept,
woke to find it pruned and
numb)

I like lying tangled
two cubs
struck to sleep by play

waking with you
alarm on snooze
enfolding you, preciously
like an origami swan

I like eating mandarin bits
from the tip of your tongue

I like kissing good-bye
cuntaste lingering

WHO'S WATCHING

Watching you
watching her
being fisted

ejaculate pulses
splashing your long feet

Watching her
my hand
flashes between your legs
tugs at your labia ring

She watches her lover
the careful gloved fister
pressing in and out
her twice-birth-cunt

Her lover smiles
watching us watching

And on the screen
the Lusty Lesbians
ooh and ahh
with dildo precision

For three dollars
who's watching
the video?

LABIA-LAUGHING

you
make me
smell cunt
while studying
you make me
crawl on you
like a water buffalo
shaking its ass to shore

you make me
swan dive your muff
at the slightest
invitation
you make me
want to fuck all day
and leave the revolution
to others

you make me flirt
my body before you
as if for sacrifice:
cannibal cunts

you make me
do things
with my tongue
that even I can't write home about

you make me
strip at mid-day

you make me
sway off your hips
like an elephant's trunk

you make me
dip my fingers
in a chocolate-cream cunt
you make me
yell
scream, cuddle, couple
you make my blood bubble

you make me
clit-happy
and labia-laughing

SATURDAY SHOPPING

Fondling the zucchini
you say, shaking your head
that one
will be too big

We settle on an English cucumber
a better curve
I say

You say
where are the dried fruit?
We don plastic gloves
paw through pears and peaches
choosing ones with still sticky centres

Doesn't this one look
REAL!?
I say, holding a pear aloft in one palm

But look around, you're gone
a man nearby
spills buckwheat flour on the floor

When I find you
a stolen kiss
is disappearing into your mouth
I lick the lingering chocolate
from the corner of your lips
you stash more kisses
in a breast pocket

One last stop for fresh figs

At the check-out
kisses jab from your pocket
in an obvious way

But the cashier
just smiles
handing you change
she says
Come Again

DILDO FUCK MUFFINS

2 servings

Pre-heat body temperatures to HOT.
Cooking time approximately 5 minutes to 2 hours.

Ingredients:

DRY	WET
– 1 leather harness	– 1 teaspoon saliva (more to taste)
– 1 silicone rubber dildo	– 1 tablespoon K-Y personal lubricant (water soluble) keep at room temperature
– 1 Trojan dildo sheath	
– 1 fresh humper	
– 1 seasoned muff	
– (full-length mirror, optional)	– cunt juice ⎤ to
	– ejaculate juice ⎦ measure

Apply sheath to dildo following directions on package. Strip humper and dress with harness and sheathed dildo. Prepare seasoned muff with saliva applied generously by mouth, until moist. Slather K-Y personal lubricant over muff and dildo, making sure all parts are well greased. Combine dildo tip and muff with a few easy strokes. Press muff up against dildo. Stir constantly until muff reaches desired thickness. Check mirror periodically to gauge movements. (For more mirror recipes, see p. 443.) Bring ingredients to boiling point. When muff is hot and spurting juices, remove dildo and fold hand inside. Muff walls should spring back lightly when touched. Knead gently until done. (Don't forget to lick the bowl!)

This is the recipe your mother may have forgotten to pass on. Dildo fuck muffins can be mixed quickly if guests are arriving or baked slowly during those holiday leisure hours. Served with Devonshire cream, mango jam (see jams) or other condiments, dildo fuck muffins are always popular at parties or for that favourite Sunday breakfast in bed.

Try them! Enjoy! And pass on the recipe to a friend.

ALSO FROM *gynergy books*

- **A House Not Her Own: Stories from Beirut**, *Emily Nasrallah*.
  This internationally acclaimed Lebanese author and feminist writes about what she knows only too well: war and the civilians who live within the bombed-out shell of Beirut. ISBN 0-921881-19-3 $ 12.95

- **By Word of Mouth: Lesbians write the erotic**, *Lee Fleming (ed.)*.
  A bedside book of short fiction and poetry by thirty-one lesbian writers. Now in its second printing.
  ISBN 0-921881-06-1 $ 10.95 / $ 12.95 US

- **Each Small Step: Breaking the chains of abuse and addiction**, *Marilyn MacKinnon (ed.)*. This groundbreaking anthology contains narratives by women recovering from the traumas of childhood sexual abuse and alcohol and chemical dependency.
  ISBN 0-921881-17-7 $ 10.95

- **Friends I Never Knew**, *Tanya Lester*.
  In this finely-crafted novel, Tara exiles herself on a Greek island to write about five extraordinary women she has met from her years in the women's movement. In the process, Tara unexpectedly writes her own story. ISBN 0-921881-18-5 $ 10.95

- **Imprinting Our Image: An International Anthology by Women with Disabilities**, *Diane Driedger and Susan Gray*.
  In this first-ever international collection, 18 disabled women from every region of the globe relate their stories, each maintaining their unique cultural voice and perspective.
  ISBN 0-921881-22-3 $ 12.95

- **The Montreal Massacre**, *Marie Chalouh and Louise Malette (eds.)*.
  Feminist letters, essays and poems examine the misogyny inherent in the mass murder of fourteen women at École Polytechnique in Montreal, Quebec on December 6, 1989.
  ISBN 0-921881-14-2 $ 12.95

- **Tide Lines: Stories of change by lesbians**, *Lee Fleming (ed.)*.
  These diverse short stories explore the many faces of change—instantaneous, over-a-lifetime, subtle or cataclysmic.
  ISBN 0-921881-15-0 $ 10.95

gynergy books can be found in quality bookstores, or individual orders can be sent, prepaid, to: *gynergy books*, P.O. Box 2023, Charlottetown, PEI, Canada, C1A 7N7. Please add postage and handling ($1.50 for the first book and 75 cents for each additional book) to your order. Canadian residents add 7% GST to the total amount. GST registration number R104383120.